LOVESONG (IMPERFECT)

José Rivera

I0140121

BROADWAY PLAY PUBLISHING INC
New York
www.broadwayplaypublishing.com
info@broadwayplaypublishing.com

LOVESONG (IMPERFECT)
© Copyright 2021 José Rivera

All rights reserved. This work is fully protected under the copyright laws of the United States of America. No part of this publication may be photocopied, reproduced, stored in a retrieval system, or transmitted, in any form or by any means, electronic, mechanical, recording, or otherwise, without the prior permission of the publisher. Additional copies of this play are available from the publisher.

Written permission is required for live performance of any sort. This includes readings, cuttings, scenes, and excerpts. For amateur and stock performances, please contact Broadway Play Publishing Inc. For all other rights please contact Jamie Kaye-Phillips, U T A, Jamie. KayePhillips@unitedtalent.com.

First edition: March 2021
I S B N: 978-0-88145-893-0

Book design: Marie Donovan
Page make-up: Adobe InDesign
Typeface: Palatino

LOVESONG (IMPERFECT) was first publicly performed at the 14th Street Y in New York, running from 8-22 February 2020, produced by Planet Connections (Glory Kadigan, Producing Artistic Director; Kim Marie Jones, Assistant Producer). The cast and creative contributors were:

DELILAH .... Sara Koviak
VENEZIO ....Francesco Andolfi
DR GOPNIK...James B Kennedy

Director..José Rivera
Assistant Director..Anna Hogan
Set Designer..Izzy Fields
Costume Designer..................................Lisa Renee Jordan
Lighting Designer..Joe Novak
Prop Master .... Lytza R Colon
Sound Designer .... George Port
Composer & Violinist ....Helen Yee
Fight design .... Brandon Bogle & Conor D Mullen
Production Stage Manager...........................Cordelia Senie
Assistant Stage Manager............................. Addi Herndon
Board Operator ....Kyle Ronyecs
Crew... Alison Beth

CHARACTERS

DELILAH
VENEZIO
DR GOPNIK

For Sara

ACT ONE

(A green field)

(A Tree with little white lights instead of leaves)

(Barrels of radioactive toxic waste and other industrial debris)

(An ancient typewriter on one of the barrels)

(DELILAH fences with VENEZIO. Both are young, healthy and attractive.)

(DELILAH stabs VENEZIO in the heart. Great amounts of his blood flow.)

VENEZIO: Ayyyy! Yes! That's a really good shot, Delilah!

DELILAH: Does it hurt, honey? Are you in terrible pain?

(VENEZIO's in terrible pain.)

VENEZIO: I'd say, yeah, there's still a whole lot of terrible pain in the world!

DELILAH: *Told* you there would be, idiot. Now quit distracting me. I have a major job to do here—

VENEZIO: You're a mensch for helping me out like this. If I wasn't bleeding to death, I'd kiss you! Instead, just watch me die!

(VENEZIO staggers dramatically around the stage, trying very hard to bleed to death.)

(DELILAH watches him, exasperated.)

DELILAH: Why do I indulge him, Tree? Why do I play his little games?

(The Tree blinks in response.)

VENEZIO: You've broken my heart before. But this time it's *not* a figure of speech.

DELILAH: *You've* broken *my* heart! You're the one with the endless parade of bimbos and—

VENEZIO: Okay, we don't need to go there!

DELILAH: After all the trouble and expense we went through to get you a new heart. Which *doesn't* seem to be cutting the love mustard in the old bedroom departments, by-the-way.

(Frustrated, DELILAH leaves the stage.)

(VENEZIO watches himself bleed, calls out to DELILAH.)

VENEZIO: Every second that passes, my life-force drains away. You'll see. If this keeps up, I'll be dead by tomorrow morning.

(DELILAH enters with rolls of architectural drawings.)

DELILAH: Oh, you wish.

(DELILAH unrolls the drawings and studies them.)

(VENEZIO stops dying long enough to look the drawings, wary.)

VENEZIO: And what the hell is that?

DELILAH: Plans for the love-nest, dummy. I'm going to build it right here—next to our gorgeous Tree of Light.

(VENEZIO gives up dying.)

VENEZIO: Ugh!! Balls!! The world we live in has gone totally to *mierda*—to shit!

DELILAH: What'd you expect? Nothing's been the same since the junta came in with their fancy theories, pie-graphs, and five-year-plans.

(The sight of all the blood suddenly makes VENEZIO *panic.)*

VENEZIO: Ay, look at this blood. The mess is unprecedented!

DELILAH: You are *useless* in the arts of self-maintenance. Must I do everything myself?

*(*DELILAH *takes out a whistle.)*

VENEZIO: No, please, don't call that quack. All he's going to do is save my life and hit on you.

DELILAH: But Doctor Gopnik cured my first cold—with great skill, I might add.

*(*DELILAH *blows the whistle.)*

*(*DOCTOR GOPNIK *enters riding a bicycle. Tall, distinguished, something Eastern European or Middle Eastern about him. He's got an old fashioned doctor bag.)*

GOPNIK: Well if it isn't the beguiling Delilah. It's been far too long, my dark monster of desire.

DELILAH: Well if it isn't the worldly, handsome medicine man with the twinkly little eyeballs and excellent bedside manner.

GOPNIK: It's been far too long since I've been summoned to *your* bedside, my fetching, young paradox of love…

VENEZIO: Yo, people! In massive pain over here?!

*(*GOPNIK *parks his bicycle, goes to* VENEZIO *and looks him over.)*

GOPNIK: Another futile attempt to take the coward's way out, I see. I've seen cases like this all over town. Everyone's having a hard time adjusting to the shitty, new zeitgeist.

VENEZIO: We were practicing murder.

GOPNIK: Why would you do such a black thing on such a shining day?

(DELILAH *resumes studying the architectural plans.*)

DELILAH: That's what I want to know. All our patterns and rhythms have changed completely since the U S government outlawed death and dying in America. Nothing means what it used to mean. It's mere chaos, I tell you.

(GOPNIK *examines* VENEZIO's *wound, the gushing blood.*)

VENEZIO: But Doctor, if all the blood runs out of me and nothing's left to feed my hungry little cells, won't they perish and send my soul to a better place?

GOPNIK: The body will just heal itself and make more cells. Everyone's afraid to break the law, even Mother Nature.

VENEZIO: That bitch is never there when you need her!

DELILAH: At least at one point, while death was still legal, time ran out, so you had a reason to do something. Some *urgency*. These days? Jesus, the only real question you can ask is: *why*, Doctor Gopnik, *why*?

GOPNIK: I may have degrees in astrology, telepathy, foot-binding, Past Lives, the Secrets of Atlantis, and Contemporary Media Studies…it don't mean I know dick.

DELILAH: Don't say that, you know *everything*, you *have* to. Your mind is what I count on in this shape-shifting world.

(GOPNIK *applies a bandage to* VENEZIO's *chest.*)

GOPNIK: That's a fine, stout heart you've got in there, young Venezio.

VENEZIO: I got it from a nice Puerto Rican kid. Delilah made me get it. To improve my penetration.

DELILAH: Who are the world's best lovers? All my Puerto Rican friends told me it's the Puerto Ricans. So I scoured the Internet until I found a donor in Brooklyn.

VENEZIO: I had the operation just before they outlawed death.

DELILAH: Venezio's new heart has made him slightly more romantic. We're getting married.

VENEZIO: We're not getting married.

DELILAH: We're getting married.

VENEZIO: We're not getting married!

DELILAH: You sleep with me all these years but you don't want to marry me. What a leech! Read poetry to me, hunt big game for me, tattoo my name on your rectum, it means nothing.

VENEZIO: I tattooed her phone number on my rectum, not her name. And let me tell you, the *pain*? Indescribable!

GOPNIK: It's so good to see that romance isn't dead in this loveless country.

DELILAH: Venezio and I have set a date.

VENEZIO: We have not!

DELILAH: And sent out invitations!

VENEZIO: *Maldita sea tu madre—what??*

DELILAH: The invitations are on pink paper.

GOPNIK: Very few colors express the futility of love like pink.

VENEZIO: So, how am I, Doctor Gopnik? Am I gonna make it?

GOPNIK: I'm afraid you're going to live the rest of your life.

VENEZIO: Shit! That bites!

DELILAH: Once an invitation is sent, honey, you can't take it back.

VENEZIO: Why do I sense a contradiction here? If everything's futile and lame and chaotic, why do you want to get married?

DELILAH: Every one knows the art of dying is a lost art. There's no music in it, no grace, no heroism of any kind. That's why we must concentrate on the lost arts of love and marriage.

GOPNIK: So, his penetration…not so much, huh?

DELILAH: A man with a death-wish isn't likely to penetrate a woman very deeply. There's always something vague and mushy about it.

(DELILAH *leaves the stage.*)

VENEZIO: What am I going to do, Doc? I want to die but The Man won't let me. And she's got future plans.

GOPNIK: Perhaps you can think of sex with Delilah as it's own form of death. Think of your orgasm as a kind of personal self-execution. Your coitus as a substitute for the soft oblivion of the grave…

(DELILAH *enters with surveying equipment and tape measure, and takes precise measurements of the space.*)

DELILAH: I try to take Venezio somewhere when we're in bed, Doc. To get him to see something new, original, and all mine. But he closes his eyes, and does his limp, little business, and never tells me what he felt or what he learned.

VENEZIO: Ain't nothing wrong with my penetration, people, end of sentence.

DELILAH: You don't know, you're not on the receiving end.

GOPNIK: Oh, ouch!

VENEZIO: Then what do you want to get married for?

DELILAH: Because we sent out the invitations!

VENEZIO: Well, I'm not showing up. Unless Doctor Gopnik removes your *larynx* and I don't have to listen to your *yap* all the rest of my days, which, as you know, are now infinite in number.

(DELILAH *continues to work on the space.*)

DELILAH: I try to give this man a gift. A chance to be part of a mystery, and take a ride to the outer edge of his own existence, where words mean nothing, and logic is a joke, and all jokes are dirty, and he doesn't have any problems with the pure biology of the act—except for the so-so penetration—but he sure falls short on the goddamn metaphysics. Meanwhile I'm flooding him with hope. I'm surrendering everything to him.

(VENEZIO *helps* DELILAH *measure the space.*)

VENEZIO: I appreciate the hope you give me. And no one makes me laugh like you do, and on paper, we're perfect for each other. Remember when we were kids and we planted that beautiful Tree together…?

DELILAH: …and how we discovered that instead of turning light into sugar, it turned light into more light!

(*The Tree blinks in response.*)

DELILAH & VENEZIO: We read books under that light.

VENEZIO: But we were kids then and we're not kids now. And I, I just don't know what's wrong with me. I think of getting married and I freeze inside…

(DELILAH *takes the tape measure away from* VENEZIO.)

DELILAH: "Freeze." Well, you just have a million excuses for everything. So many reasons to not grow up and be a man.

VENEZIO: You don't know the suffering my doubts and fears give me! All I do at night is suffer. My dreams—the ones of living in this house—beat the living shit

outta me every night. I wake up each morning bruised
from head to toe…

(He gets a strange look on his face: an epiphany.)

…h-hey…*wait.* If the government can cancel death…
then why can't they cancel pain and suffering?

(The typewriter glows with magical light.)

*(*VENEZIO *stares at it, scheming.)*

VENEZIO: That's it. I'm going to petition this
government and demand they either outlaw pain and
suffering—which totally includes shitty, unwanted
marriages—which, as we know, will now literally *last
forever*—or the junta has to bring back death, forthwith!

(Inspired, he starts typing.)

"Dear Assholes in the Gov-ern-ment ..."

*(*DELILAH *looks at* VENEZIO*, angry.)*

DELILAH: Can you believe this joker?

GOPNIK: The outlawing of death in America has
screwed me royal. Death made things *fun.* Practicing
medicine was life on a knife's edge—one wrong move
and your patient paid the ultimate price. Now, there's
no risk, no danger. And if they outlaw suffering and
pain too, I'll be just another tall, handsome, over-
educated man with no actual usefulness.

VENEZIO: "I am a middle-class, tax-paying slob with
working class roots: you might call me the very
backbone of this country."

DELILAH: As long as we're human, we're going to make
each other suffer, doctor, so stop your whining. You
will end up with a fortune made from the countless
tears of other people. And maybe you'll finally be
happy.

VENEZIO: "So you assholes have to listen to me!"

(It goes from day to night, back to day again.)

DELILAH: Ah! The wedding date approaches. My work schedule accelerates! Excuse me, gentlemen!

(DELILAH *leaves the stage.*)

(VENEZIO *writes, laughing.*)

(GOPNIK *takes out a flask and drinks.*)

GOPNIK: Is she right? Will money and fame fill the aching void in the center of my being? God knows love has not yet filled the abyss within. No matter how hard I try.

(VENEZIO *only half-listens to* GOPNIK.)

VENEZIO: So hard to believe, hot *papi chulo* like you...

GOPNIK: It's because I've mausoleumed myself in libraries, piling on more and more deadly degrees in this lame search for meaning. I confess it: I've had too many books and too few freaky nights of love!

(DELILAH *enters with building material, glances at* VENEZIO *typing.*)

DELILAH: You're wasting your time! They don't listen to the people!

(*Despondent,* GOPNIK *goes to* DELILAH *as she begins to lay out the walls of the house.*)

GOPNIK: Just imagine what I could've learned, of real value, if I had only been turning the moist, yielding pages of the opposite sex, instead of the dusty old tomes of Aristotle.

DELILAH: Yes, Doctor Gopnik, you would have learned to cure even yourself.

GOPNIK: *Connection.* Yes, deep and satisfying *connection.* Within that gentle syringe is the vaccine I seek, dear Delilah. What are you doing for dinner?

DELILAH: Busy. But thank you. For a moment there, I understood what it meant to feel *desired.* By a *man.*

(GOPNIK *looks at* VENEZIO, *smiles.*)

GOPNIK: Take notes, chump.

(VENEZIO *laughs, typing faster and faster.*)

VENEZIO: I don't have time. I'm too busy stickin' it to the Man!

DELILAH: This house is going to rock! I've always wanted a little house. In my adolescence I drifted from man to man and place to place, like the lonely moon. Then, as now, I saw the nightmares of our future and I described them to my lovers with uncanny relish and in vivid 3-D. But no lover could put up with my visions!

GOPNIK: I would be honored to put up with them. If you would only let me.

DELILAH: Dear doctor, you were my pediatrician. You saw me naked when I was six days old. Fuckin' gross.

GOPNIK: All the bitches I like say that.

DELILAH: This house is going to be a temple, and a haven, and a castle, and a circus, and a rock, and a dream, and a fuck-place, and where you get dressed to play all the roles of your life and where you get cleansed to be your true self again. How cool is that? And after Venezio and I are wed, we will move into this house and produce amazing babies with my good looks, my overwhelming intelligence, and my joyous sense of gloom.

(VENEZIO *stops typing.*)

VENEZIO: And me? What do I contribute to this nuclear family?

DELILAH: Sperm cells, like *many.*

VENEZIO: I feel like I'm being used for my fertilizing ability but little else. That really blows, Delilah!

GOPNIK: Fool! That's not how you talk to a force capable of inspiring the poems of Tupac!

DELILAH: Thank you, Doctor Gopnik, for making him understand.

VENEZIO: I understand so very little right now, I really do. I feel—I feel—I feel—!

(He suddenly jumps to his feet and salsas around the stage like a man possessed.)

(It spooks him out.)

What the fuck was *that?*

(GOPNIK sidles up to DELILAH.)

GOPNIK: Are you sure you won't have dinner? Because he will never understand. He has no intuitive powers. All he knows is what his senses and experience tell him. And we all know, of all the forces in the world, the testimony of our senses and experience is the weakest one.

(The outline of the house is complete. DELILAH looks at it with great satisfaction.)

DELILAH: Living room, bed room, rumpus room and nursery. Come look, Venezio!

(VENEZIO looks at the shape on the floor, apprehensive.)

VENEZIO: *Ay Dios mio, que jodienda.*

DELILAH: From these rooms we will watch the pretty lights of the apocalypse. With time we will fill these vague, spacious rooms with the funk-flavored memories of our pungent love. And those odors will mingle with the dreams of our unfulfilled desire— because love is finite, but desire is endless, especially *mine*—and when they come together, they will make a warm soup of nostalgia and longing. Oh, it will be exquisite in its breathtaking futility and sadness!

VENEZIO: Why do I feel a seismic shift about to occur in the fragile water of my bowels?

DELILAH: Venezio, you drama queen, take my hand.

VENEZIO: Why?

(DELILAH *grabs his hand and he stops dancing.*)

DELILAH: Doctor Gopnik, I do believe you have a degree in theology and are able to marry us?

GOPNIK: Oy. Uhm. This presents a problem for me because I don't fucking really want to…

(VENEZIO *lets her hand go, runs to one of the swords and tries to stab himself again.*)

(VENEZIO *gives up stabbing himself. He goes sullenly to* DELILAH.)

VENEZIO: My Puerto Rican heart is about to burst.

(DELILAH *takes* VENEZIO's *hand.*)

DELILAH: You may begin, good doctor.

GOPNIK: But, alas, I'm a fool for love and if you asked me to dismember myself in your name, I would scatter my happy organs to all corners of this polluted world and sing your praises as I do.

DELILAH: I do! I do!

VENEZIO: What just happened?!

DELILAH: In a country where no one dies anymore, what does it mean to pledge your love forever? It means our vows have greater strength, Venezio.

VENEZIO: What vows?

DELILAH: I promise to do this, I promise to do that, I promise the whole dang thing! You may now kiss the bride!

VENEZIO: Wait—

(DELILAH *kisses* VENEZIO.)

DELILAH: Maybe being a married man will improve your penetration, dear.

VENEZIO: Who's a married man—?

(DELILAH *sings the wedding march.*)

(DELILAH *and the confused* VENEZIO *march around the stage.*)

(GOPNIK *throws rose petals and quietly weeps.*)

GOPNIK: I remember the day I realized I was mortal. I was in the boy's room at school, taking a leak, looking down at the golden shower. I was pissing on a cockroach lying on its back in the latrine, drowning it slowly in my warm pee as it weakly kicked it's tiny dying stick-legs. And that's when I realized that I was never going to leave this world alive. That I had to die—and it was probably going to hurt a lot and be full of humiliation, just like this bug. And I began to wonder what form my final pain and shame would take: strangulation? Stabbing? Eaten by dogs? Oh, how I hate pain and suffering! How afraid I am of unknown things! How unfair it is that we're put on earth only to leave it in the most miserable and painful way!

(He blows his nose.)

A few days ago, I learned I didn't have to be afraid of that any more, and I was happy for a time. But today, as I look at you, Delilah, married to that sniveling man-child, I feel a fear far worse than any I ever felt before.

(DELILAH *and* VENEZIO *stop marching. She looks at him.*)

DELILAH: Venezio, my husband, I know you're not perfect.

VENEZIO: What gave it away?

DELILAH: All of it. But here's the shocker: neither am I.

VENEZIO: No, don't say that! I count on your perfection to get me through the day!

DELILAH: And we live in a scary world. And we don't know what's going to happen to us. Will they start to ration the air? Will they put a new tax on sunlight? Will the oceans go on strike? They say that gravity has fallen out of love with the earth and there might be consequences. Can we survive all that, Venezio?

VENEZIO: How would I know? I love you with a purchased heart.

GOPNIK: Send in your petition, Venezio. Make those fools in government know that we want death back.

VENEZIO: Yes, we want death back!

GOPNIK: We want death with a vengeance!

GOPNIK & VENEZIO: We want death!!

(VENEZIO *hits a key on the typewriter. It goes ding! Fireworks boom in the distance.*)

(*Black out*)

END OF ACT ONE

ACT TWO

(Two days later.)

(A barrel of radioactive waste serves as a kitchen table, with two chairs, breakfast food, and a newspaper.)

*(*DELILAH *and* VENEZIO *eat breakfast.)*

*(*VENEZIO *wears a guayabera.)*

(A tense silence between the two of them, then:)

DELILAH: You keep me up all night with your snoring.

VENEZIO: These *huevos* are exhausting and you fart in your sleep.

DELILAH: Your feet are so cold they drive the blood from my legs when you touch them with your nasty, uneven toes.

VENEZIO: Obviously any chance I had for a little privacy and personal space has been blown to pieces because of you.

DELILAH: I won't indulge your amazing need for secrecy.

VENEZIO: Why do I need to share every thought in my head with you?

DELILAH: Why would you want to keep your thoughts from me?

*(*VENEZIO *cries.)*

*(*DELILAH *just looks at* VENEZIO.)*

(VENEZIO stops crying.)

VENEZIO: My tears mean nothing to you.

DELILAH: You cry in order to control me.

VENEZIO: You lack empathy.

DELILAH: The world is much bigger than the sum of your petty grievances and desires, little man.

VENEZIO: I was supposed to *be* your world.

DELILAH: Until I started to grow up.

VENEZIO: But you weren't supposed to change.

DELILAH: And you were.

(Tense moment of silence)

VENEZIO: I think we need a change of pace. Maybe a trip? A little get-away to help me breathe.

(DELILAH holds up a newspaper.)

DELILAH: It's not safe to travel. International tensions are at an all-time high. Something bad's going to happen, I feel it. Something really big.

VENEZIO: But a change of scenery could inspire a change of *corazon*—heart!

DELILAH: It's the same everywhere: a lack of color in the sky, no bird-songs, a sad, green moon, and fish that tastes like mostly plastic.

(Beat)

VENEZIO: Remember how much fun we used to have trying to stab each other?

(This brings a sad smile to DELILAH.)

DELILAH: I can't even remember where we keep the swords.

VENEZIO: How long have we been married now?

DELILAH: It's day two, isn't it?

VENEZIO: Oh, happy honeymoon! This marriage totally rocks!

(VENEZIO *jumps to his feet. He salsas around the stage.*)

DELILAH: We will never arrive at consensus if you can't stand still!

VENEZIO: It's not me! It's my Puerto Rican heart! And why do I have memories of the projects in Boerum Hill? Why do I want you to call me Papo??

DELILAH: And I thought after you gave up your quest to die, things would be better with you. That there'd be this little thing between us called *Stability*.

VENEZIO: Who says I've given up!? Huh?! You think I want this for all the rest of eternity?! This—endless— morbid—*stability*?

(*He runs to the radioactive barrels and drinks the radioactive waste.*)

(*He is suddenly very still.*)

(DELILAH *looks at* VENEZIO, *worried.*)

VENEZIO: *Coño*, that shit burns.

(VENEZIO *falls to the ground and writhes in terrible pain.*)

(DELILAH *watches him a few moments, shaking her head.*)

(DELILAH *takes out her whistle and blows it.*)

(GOPNIK *appears on his bicycle, doctor bag in hand.*)

DELILAH: He refuses to face reality. Again.

GOPNIK: Reality is an ugly whore with a mustache caked with the left-over love-juice of last night's john. Who can blame the boy for not wanting to look at that?

DELILAH: You men sure like to stick together, don't you?

GOPNIK: Ah, these days we must all stick together. Have you read the papers? Rumors of war! Have you listened to the earth? The groaning of the earth's digestive tract filled with plastic and poison!

(VENEZIO *groans in pain.*)

VENEZIO: Obviously this is a minor tummy ache, otherwise it would be impossible to explain the total lack of *haste* and *urgency* on the part of the good doctor.

(DELILAH *and* GOPNIK *go to the writhing* VENEZIO.)

GOPNIK: This has become chronic with you, these pathetic attempts to take the coward's way out.

DELILAH: That's telling him.

VENEZIO: Oh, nice to see you too, Doc! Fucking pull up a chair!

(GOPNIK *opens his doctor's bag, takes out his tools and examines* VENEZIO.)

GOPNIK: How's the heart?

VENEZIO: I often find myself humming Tito Puente songs and yearning for *arroz con habichuelas* and I don't even speak Spanish. *!Ay carajo!* Who said that?!

GOPNIK: Interesting. Take off your *guayabera*.

VENEZIO: I'm wearing a *guayabera*?!

DELILAH: What this house needs—besides a stable male figure and many consecutive nights of sweaty love-making—is more furniture.
(*She leaves the stage.*)

GOPNIK: So, my friend, it seems the U S government never granted your request to bring back death.

VENEZIO: They are deaf to the wishes of the people, Doctor Gopnik.

GOPNIK: Because we don't scream loud enough, is the problem.

VENEZIO: *!VIVA LA REVOLUCION! !MUERTE A LOS PERROS Y DEMONIOS DEL CAPITALISMO!!*

GOPNIK: Side effects. They really blow my mind. Open.

(VENEZIO *opens his mouth.*)

(GOPNIK *looks in with a flashlight.*)

(DELILAH *enters with chairs. She puts them in the house.*)

DELILAH: Bad?

GOPNIK: There are a lot of things down there I wish I had never seen.

VENEZIO: Sorry, Doc. I hold on to stuff.

(GOPNIK *gives* VENEZIO *pills.*)

GOPNIK: These pills will neutralize the radioactive waste in your system. If they don't, well, your screams of pain will be loud enough to awaken the dead.

(VENEZIO *takes the pills and feels instantly better.*)

VENEZIO: You're a mensch.

DELILAH: Wait, people! I sense another sale!

(DELILAH *leaves the stage.*)

(VENEZIO *pulls* GOPNIK *aside.*)

VENEZIO: So what do I do about—*thing*? I've known her since we were babies on the playground. She taught me the two-times table and put her tongue on my lips to lick off the excess cherry lollipops my mother gave me each morning instead of breakfast. Our games of doctor went on for long afternoons as the jealous blue sky watched and never said a word to our parents. I knew her body better than mine and watched her slow adolescence take away her innocence and every day my first thought upon awakening was: I want to see my Delilah!

GOPNIK: You guys played, like—*doctor*?

VENEZIO: All during our adolescence I pursued her and she didn't want me because her teen-girl hormones were tuned to bad boys and motorcycle jocks and tattooed knaves, and look at me, I don't even have chin hair. Ah, but I persisted and she finally said yes—but as soon as I had her, something went wrong. The chase was over, the adventure ended, I was bored and distracted. So we broke up and…are you even listening to me, Doc?

GOPNIK: Didn't I see this plot in a telenovela?

VENEZIO: Yes, my suffering is archetypal, good sir, yes! We broke up and I found comfort in the arms of a variety of hot and completely fucked up crazy bitches. But I missed my best friend. And after a good deal of groveling, she's taken me back. See my problem? Now that I have her, I miss yearning for her! Oh, there's nothing as painful or as sweet as yearning for love.

GOPNIK: Alas, I am no stranger to this feeling.

VENEZIO: What you and I share, good doctor, is a malaise of the worse kind. The original ache in the heart of every man: the pain of desiring the thing we cannot have.

(A newspaper flies on stage. GOPNIK *catches it and reads.)*

GOPNIK: We're going to war! The corporations—I mean our country—have mobilized in a spectacular show of force. The corporations—I mean our country—have decided that since we've outlawed death in America we can go to war with the rest of the world and be assured a swift, absolute and final victory.

VENEZIO: But if no one can kill us, why would we feel threatened? And if we can't die in battle, can you really call it war?
(He gets a thought.)
Say, *w-wait…*

(DELILAH *enters with a big comfy chair.*)

DELILAH: I got us a big comfy chair!

VENEZIO: Have you heard the great news, Delilah?
We're going to war with the world!

DELILAH: What kind of lamps do you think we should
get?

VENEZIO: And I've figured out a route to my salvation:
I'm going to leave the U S and go to some third-world
Latin country where death is not only possible, but a
very high probability.

DELILAH: But. I just went to *Ikea*. And besides, you're
American, you can't die anywhere.

VENEZIO: But. My heart is *Puerto Rican,* which was
illegally invaded by the Yankee imperialists in
1898 and whose pure *Boriqua* soul has always been
independent of North American corporate interests! *Ay
si!* The very organ that keeps me alive is free.

DELILAH: But—*Ikea.*

(VENEZIO *takes* DELILAH's *hand. Looks deep into her eyes*)

VENEZIO: No, Delilah, I'm sorry. This isn't working. Us.

DELILAH: That's the first time you've ever said the
word "us" to my face.

VENEZIO: Actually I've never said it before, even to
myself.

DELILAH: Oh, sweet.

VENEZIO: I don't know what's wrong with me.
You're beautiful and brave. You're so far ahead of me
intellectually speaking it's not even funny anymore.
You have spiritual and cosmic dimensions I can only
guess at. And you make the best cannolis.

DELILAH: But Ikea is Swedish for commitment,
Venezio.

VENEZIO: But I *haven't*—I still *can't*—words *fail* to—I'm
brutishly *inarticulate* right now—

(DELILAH *lets* VENEZIO's *hand go.*)

DELILAH: Doctor Gopnik, can you leave us alone a
moment? Venezio and I are going to have a deep and
nuanced conversation about the perpetual crisis in our
relationship.

GOPNIK: Absolutely, my heart!
(He hides behind the magic Tree, a happy man.)
Oh, I must be dreaming this…!

(DELILAH *turns to* VENEZIO.)

DELILAH: YOU'RE AN ASSHOLE! AND A TOTAL
BABY-MAN, PUSSIFIED, CHICKEN-SHIT NEUROTIC
FUCK-WAD!
(She has to fight to keep from crying.)
Doctor Gopnik, can you come back here please?

(GOPNIK *rushes back to* DELILAH's *side.*)

GOPNIK: At your service!

DELILAH: He's leaving me. Why does this have to
happen, Doctor Gopnik?

GOPNIK: When a man says he can't do something,
women should really listen to that because it's one of
those few times men are being, like, honest.

DELILAH: Oh you're no help, get out of my sight! You
men really *do* stick together! Traitor!

(GOPNIK hides behind the magic tree, tail between his legs.)

VENEZIO: Delilah, it's no use—

DELILAH: Don't you even want to see how comfy
this chair is? Don't you want to imagine yourself the
patriarch of a beautiful little family, sitting on a comfy
chair after a hard day's night, your temples rubbed by
your loving wife, after she comes home from *her* high-

paying job, artisanal beers brought to you by the kids, Buster and Jennifer? And then we have some really hot sex?

(VENEZIO *sits in the comfy chair. Thinks about it.*)

(*Enjoys the image for a moment*)

VENEZIO: On the one hand, a castle where I make the laws and little versions of me obey without sniveling or dissent. On the other hand, a miserable, fly-infested death in a lonely third-world country as immortal Americans drop napalm on my ass from thirty thousand feet.

DELILAH: Yes, darling.

(VENEZIO *jumps out of the comfy chair.*)

VENEZIO: *!Ay mi madre!* I can't!

DELILAH: You do this to me every time, Venezio. Since that first day on the playground.

VENEZIO: Maybe that was a clue?

DELILAH: But I didn't know I was a girl until later when I saw you naked. Remember that day? Our moms took us swimming. You took off your swimsuit and jumped in the water with me and told me to take off mine. I saw the little fish between your legs and something happened in my brain—my mind did a little dance! I laughed when I saw it. And I knew I was a girl and you'd be mine some day.

VENEZIO: I can't take responsibility for your sick, childish memories.

DELILAH: No? Then what about my *chemistry*, which you mangled and twisted and re-built to be a perfect fit to yours?

VENEZIO: You ask a provocative question—

DELILAH: What about the space you created in my mind where your voice sits and you whisper to me and I can't tell half the time which voice is talking, mine or yours?

VENEZIO: That one's good too, *coño*.

DELILAH: What about my *time* which has been divided to not only include you, but to give you the best slices, the brightest hours, of my day?

VENEZIO: I knew, if I got into a battle of words, you'd clean my closet.

DELILAH: Well, guess what, we are *entombed* in words, sweet man. Words are the mausoleum, the cold labyrinth, the bloody necropolis of our love right now. *(She collapses on the comfy chair, face in her hands.)*

(VENEZIO looks at her, unsure what to do.)

VENEZIO: I'm unsure what to do.

DELILAH: Just go to Guatemala and die. There's the exit.

(Now that he's gotten permission to leave, VENEZIO can't go. He goes to DELILAH and takes her hand.)

(Surprised, DELILAH holds his hand and looks at him.)

(A newspaper flies in, GOPNIK catches it and reads.)

(DELILAH and VENEZIO do not react: they focus solely on their intertwined hands.)

GOPNIK: Our unkillable forces have been spreading mayhem in the name of freedom to all parts of the world. Soon it will all be ours. Every toxic heap in every third world country. Every jail cell in every hole-in-the ground police station. Every inch of razor wire around every refugee camp. Every dank latrine on every beach in the tropics. Every dead species. Our glorious men and women will soon be planting the

flags of liberty firmly into the up-turned assholes of
countless non-American casualties.

(Another newspaper flies onstage. GOPNIK *catches it and
reads.)*

GOPNIK: Well! It's over! The war is done and it looks
like we won the whole dang shootin' match!

(This gets DELILAH's *and* VENEZIO's *attention.)*

GOPNIK: A moment of silence for the earth and for
human history itself.

(A moment of silence)

Now there's all that empty space out there. On tracts of
land that used to be called things like Brazil and India.
We Americans will have to multiply and re-populate
the earth. Eventually, everywhere we go will look like
Dayton, Ohio. Everyone will look like us—all history,
all ethics, all hair styles, all human behavior. There
will only be one passport for the whole world. One
nauseating easy-listening sound-track.

VENEZIO: That, sure as shit, is depressing.

DELILAH: But think of all that empty space. Now we
will have to make babies at a heart-pounding rate.

GOPNIK: Yes, reproduction will now be mandatory in
every town, you mark my words.

(Another newspaper flies onstage. DELILAH *catches it and
reads.)*

DELILAH: You called it, Doctor Gopnik.

GOPNIK: Splendid! And me without a girlfriend!

DELILAH: There are tremendous penalties for those of
us who don't pop them out fast enough.

(She goes into the bedroom, newly energized.)

Venezio, you and I need to get busy or we'll be in
violation of our nation's trust. Drop those pants!

(It becomes night. The moon is greenish.)

(DELILAH waits in the bedroom.)

(VENEZIO looks at the moon, stalling.)

VENEZIO: The poor moon. All she can do is watch us as the oceans convulse and we make the same grand mistakes again and again. Her green isn't the color of envy, it's the raw sickness she feels as her sister earth is shredded like a breakfast cereal and fed to the generals and accountants. *Ay, que barbaridad!*

(VENEZIO salsas into the bedroom. He and DELILAH look at each other.)

(DELILAH touches VENEZIO's face.)

DELILAH: I will finish this house. And it will have walls of iron and bullets. I will keep the world's pain and suffering away if it kills me.

(VENEZIO touches DELILAH's face.)

VENEZIO: I've never felt safer and more terrified in my life. Like the man who chopped down the last tree on Easter Island.

(A newspaper flies on stage. GOPNIK catches it. Can't believe what he reads.)

GOPNIK: Well, my boy, it looks like this typewriter of yours has magic powers. The junta received your brilliantly phrased petition demanding the return of death. And Congress just voted to change the laws. Death is back in America with a vengeance, my boy.

(VENEZIO's chest explodes in blood—his old fencing wound is back. He screams.)

DELILAH: Ay, Venezio!

VENEZIO: That's a really good shot, Delilah!

(DELILAH goes to him and holds him, trying to stanch the blood.)

DELILAH: Doctor Gopnik!

(VENEZIO *grabs his stomach and screams again. He goes into convulsions.*)

VENEZIO: I can't believe I actually drank that shit!!

(DELILAH *holds* VENEZIO *as his convulsions continue.*)

(GOPNIK *tries everything he knows to save him.*)

(*The convulsions slowly subside and* VENEZIO *dies.*)

(GOPNIK *looks at* DELILAH.)

GOPNIK: I'm so sorry, my dark paradox of sorrow, he's gone…

(DELILAH *is too shocked to speak.*)

(*Black out*)

END OF ACT TWO

ACT THREE

(A few days later)

(The house has white, unpainted walls. There are cans of paint, brushes and rollers.)

(DELILAH, dressed in funereal black, wanders the stage like a ghost.)

DELILAH: Venezio! Do you hear that sound? Listen. That's the sound of the earth's rotation. That rusty, squeaky spinning. It's so hard to hear sometimes. It sounds like crickets? Or rustling leaves? The noise is so primal and far away and sad. You can only hear it when you're absolutely alone in the world. When all your loved ones are gone or silent. That's me right now. I don't hear you, dear Venezio. Not your laughter or that painful little sigh you make after making love with me. I don't hear your sarcasm or your evasions and cheap jokes.

(VENEZIO, now dead and slightly transparent, appears on stage in another dimension. He watches DELILAH with an odd detachment.)

(He speaks in a whisper, as if he doesn't want to be heard.)

VENEZIO: Cheap jokes?

DELILAH: You've broken free. You've escaped my arms and flown to older dimensions and erased your presence in our biosphere and left me to wander the dumb, unfinished house like a weak wind.

VENEZIO: Those walls need some color.

DELILAH: I've been trying to hear the echoes of your words, hoping they'd still be bouncing around this tired house like magic rubber balls. Sometimes I think I hear those echoes—your voice still attached to the space around me, our space, our haven. I try to chase your echoes and catch them and stick them in my ear and hope they wander down to my heart and fill it, fill it, fill it with you! But I think I'm only dreaming those things.

VENEZIO: Delilah you need to get a grip.

DELILAH: But no, in my complete loneliness, all I hear is the rusted spin of the world, monotonous and shrill. They say only dogs and crazy people can hear that. I'm afraid that if I listen to it too much, for too long, that I will really lose my mind, dear Venezio.

VENEZIO: Dear dead Venezio, who was a total ass in life!

DELILAH: Yes he was an ass sometimes…uhm…what?

(VENEZIO *whispers.*)

VENEZIO: Nothing! I didn't say—

DELILAH: God, I'm losing it. I can't eat. I can't stand to look at these unpainted walls and think of their potential, all the things they were supposed to represent. The babies, too!

VENEZIO: Buster and Jennifer!

DELILAH: Jesus, Venezio, you ass, why did you have to write that stupid petition?

VENEZIO: Stupid Venezio.

DELILAH: Since death has returned to America…it's been an epidemic. Day and night, the guilt of our crimes, the stress of owning too much, the pain of being owned by our things, the fear of aging, the quest for perfection, the hunt for More and Better, the noise of constant communication…all of it's crashed down on our heads and everywhere, Americans are taking their own lives in unprecedented numbers.

(DELILAH *picks up a knife. She looks at its long, shiny edge, contemplating the possibilities.*)

VENEZIO: Bad idea, Delilah!

DELILAH: Why?

VENEZIO: Because!

(DELILAH *looks around, a little spooked.*)

DELILAH: Wait. Who am I talking to?

VENEZIO: No one!

DELILAH: I'm losing my blessed mind. I couldn't stand that. Even when I've had nothing, I've had the ability to think straight and form perfect sentences. That's the last straw!

(DELILAH *takes the knife and puts it to her wrist.*)

(VENEZIO *rushes to stop Delilah. Before he can get to her—*)

(GOPNIK *rides in on his bicycle wearing a brand new, expensive suit, looking sharp, happy and prosperous.*)

GOPNIK: Delilah! My soul's grief! My heart's illusion!

(VENEZIO *quickly backs off.*)

(DELILAH *puts the knife down. Strikes a nonchalant pose.*)

(Unseen by DELILAH, VENEZIO *paints the upstage walls, during the following.*)

DELILAH: Hiya, Doctor Gopnik.

GOPNIK: How are you today?

DELILAH: I'm fine, how are you?

(GOPNIK *eyes* DELILAH, *not sure he's buying this act.*)

GOPNIK: No complaints. What's new?

DELILAH: Oh, not much, what's new with you?

GOPNIK: Oh, you know, this and that.

DELILAH: Me too, this and that!

GOPNIK: You're still wearing black.

DELILAH: Seems to fit the mood around here.

GOPNIK: Have you left the house today?

DELILAH: Tomorrow I promise to leave the house.

GOPNIK: That's what you said yesterday.

DELILAH: Then I guess I lied to you, huh?

GOPNIK: How long do you think you can keep this up?

DELILAH: I'm stuck in a loop, I guess, big, stupid loop!

GOPNIK: Bad place to be stuck.

DELILAH: Can't seem to help it.

GOPNIK: Are you even trying?

DELILAH: Not so much.

GOPNIK: Because the loop is comfortable—this infinite circle of hell you're in. It's familiar and easy. Because every time he broke your heart in the past, this is where you went. So for you, it's like coming home. But this time he's not coming back. The challenge is to break that cycle, my angel. To break it wide open!

(DELILAH *looks at her knife, with the same longing to use it.*)

DELILAH: I was actually kinda thinking that myself, good doctor.

GOPNIK: So you'll do it? You'll end this unseemly, indulgent little funeral? You'll break things wide open?

DELILAH: Oh, wide, wide open, sir!

GOPNIK: I'm so glad to hear you say this. This country needs a resurgence of feel-good optimism. That's what I'm all about these days. You know why?

(DELILAH *shakes her head no and puts her hand around the knife's handle.*)

GOPNIK: America is a more beautiful place now that death has returned. Though it's mostly the poor who are dying. But, no matter, life has urgency again. There are time-limits to all our ambitions. Biological clocks are ticking again. Don't you hear that sound? The urgent tick-tick-tick of your uterus?

DELILAH: Doctor Gopnik, I have never given you a reason to hope for my love, have I?

GOPNIK: No, you've actually been pretty consistent about that—

DELILAH: But now that I'm a grieving widow you think that as soon as I see you I'm going to want to strip myself naked and join my hips to yours and take you within me in some funky, biological explosion of flesh and pleasure.

GOPNIK: Something like that, yeah.

DELILAH: You must think I'm a machine without a heart.

GOPNIK: No, no, nothing like that. You're an oracle, a geyser, you're life itself. That's why I can't stand to see you like this—

(DELILAH *lifts the knife over her head.*)

DELILAH: I won't be this way for long…!

GOPNIK: What are you doing with that!?

DELILAH: Oh, I have a plan. It's a good plan. It's going to solve all my problems, you see?

(DELILAH *puts the knife to her wrist.*)

(The sight freezes GOPNIK *with fear.)*

GOPNIK: Okay. Delilah...*deep breath now...*

DELILAH: Don't worry, Doctor Gopnik, I'm completely lucid.

GOPNIK: This is not where this story needs to go!

DELILAH: Wanna bet? I'm going to burn this house to the ground, then I'm going to slash myself in a hundred different little places like a fucking Frida Kahlo painting and throw myself on the flames.

GOPNIK: Give me the knife—

DELILAH: Take it from me. Come on, here it is, take it! Bet you can't, Doc, bet you can't! Ha! Ha! Ha!

GOPNIK: Please, I'm not psychologically equipped for extreme moments of human irrationality.

DELILAH: Tough balls!

GOPNIK: You'd really *do* this, Delilah, for that boy? That immature, on-again, off-again, heart-breaking boy?

DELILAH: That boy was the love of my life, sir!

GOPNIK: The one who's penetration wasn't very good?

DELILAH: Yes that would be the one!

GOPNIK: The one who didn't want to marry you?

DELILAH: The one who just died. Trouble is the house still smells like him. I find strands of his hair on his pillow. I'm even beginning to appreciate his salsa dancing and juvenile fear of commitment. Yes, the one I just buried. The one whose eyeholes are being eaten by worms. The eyes I'm going to miss the rest of my life.

GOPNIK: Man forgets pain.

DELILAH: I don't think I'll ever forget this pain, Doctor Gopnik, even after I'm gone. I don't think I can and I don't think I want to…

(DELILAH's *self-restraint finally breaks and she cries.*)

(GOPNIK *easily takes the knife from* DELILAH.)

GOPNIK: Let me spend the night, please. I can heal you.

DELILAH: I'll be okay. Really. I don't want you to stay or worry about me or anything.

GOPNIK: Promise you're not going to do anything stupid and I'll go.

DELILAH: I promise. You're sweet. I know you care about me and it's comforting. But I need you to go.

(GOPNIK *looks at* DELILAH *as she gets her crying under control and tries to smile reassuringly.*)

(GOPNIK *kisses* DELILAH *on the forehead, tucks the knife into his belt, and exits on his bicycle.*)

(DELILAH *is alone.*)

(*The sun goes down and night hits the stage.*)

(DELILAH *wipes her eyes. She turns upstage, sees the wall that is suddenly half-painted—and screams.*)

(VENEZIO *looks at* DELILAH *and smiles.*)

VENEZIO: In the dimension where I exist, there is very little white. Everything is turquoise or amber or cerise or electric lime—and decorated within an inch of its life. It's like the whole universe is Mexico City!

DELILAH: God. Help. Me.

VENEZIO: And there's constant music and noise. It's not exactly a party but there's no sleep. It's like a universal caffeine high.

DELILAH: No, it's okay if I lose my mind. I don't really need to think anymore.

VENEZIO: But you get stripped of a lot in the afterlife. Things that made you human—like fear, hunger, tension, the quiet panic of every day life. These things are zeroed out in this dimension. It's not exactly peace because you do get to keep your memories. And we know how tormenting memory can be. But you're no longer so attached to them. They no longer rule your existence.

DELILAH: I never knew insanity could be so informative.

VENEZIO: You don't want to fight old fights, or right old wrongs, or complete old conversations, or finish old dreams. But it's not without action. There are those out here who spend all their time studying the inside of the atom. While others like to count the fugitive stars, one by one. Me? I think maybe I'll paint these walls for my beloved.

DELILAH: Whatever is fine with me, little ghost, because you're not really here, and I'm insane right now, and what's weird is I don't actually care.

VENEZIO: Delilah. My silly. You haven't lost your mind.

DELILAH: Oh yes I have. Because yesterday I opened a gash in the earth, and lay my beloved into it, and couldn't feel or do anything as strangers covered the gash with dirt and took my beloved away. And today I'm standing in my bedroom talking to a wall that's painting itself. And when the light is just right, if I squint and catch the perfect twilight angle…I think I can see my Venezio.

VENEZIO: Delilah, you can see your Venezio. I'm back.

DELILAH: I don't want to hear those words, not even from a hallucination—there's too much hope in them.

(VENEZIO *holds* DELILAH *and she gasps.*)

DELILAH: You don't have any body temperature.

VENEZIO: You've got enough for the two of us.

(GOPNIK *sneaks back on stage. He has binoculars.*)

GOPNIK: Not that I don't trust you…

(GOPNIK *sits outside the house and spies on* DELILAH, *growing more upset and agitated as the scene continues.*)

DELILAH: How come, when you were alive, you never got this close to me?

VENEZIO: I was stupid and male. Oh, maybe that's the same thing.

DELILAH: Do I look different in your dimension?

VENEZIO: Slightly. I can see your molecules.

DELILAH: You're looking at my molecules? Bad boy!

VENEZIO: I can see the bonds of energy that hold your atoms together. I even see a little anti-matter in you!

DELILAH: Do you see my soul?

VENEZIO: I see something—it's slowly burning, but it's not a fire exactly, and it's inexhaustible, and it's somewhere in this region.

(VENEZIO *touches her heart and she gasps again.*)

DELILAH: I don't really feel that, in the normal way we understand the word "feel", but I know you're there.

VENEZIO: My condition forces many interesting questions regarding what we mean when we use the word "there".

DELILAH: I wonder, when a person is insane, am I allowed to be happy too?

VENEZIO: I'm sorry I had to die to grow up and really understand our love for each other.

DELILAH: This is a really beautiful hallucination I'm having right now, don't spoil it with negativity.

VENEZIO: You know what we should do? We should finish the house.

DELILAH: Yes! Let's paint the walls together.

(DELILAH *and* VENEZIO *begin to paint the walls of the house.*)

(GOPNIK *angrily throws down his binoculars.*)

GOPNIK: Over my trembling dead body, kids!
(*He goes to the magic typewriter.*)
(*He begins to type a letter.*)
"Dear Assholes in the Government. I own huge amounts of stock in many formidable multinational corporations. You might say I'm the very backbone of this nation."

VENEZIO: Out in my dimension, colors and sounds and tastes kind of mingle together. Out here, you can feel red, you can see B-flat, you can caress the taste of oranges, you can sing the definition of flight and smell laughter!

DELILAH: I want to visit your dimension and all its possibilities.

(GOPNIK *types faster.*)

GOPNIK: Yeah! I'm really stickin' it to the Man!

VENEZIO: But what you can't do out there…you can't make life. With all the crazy new abilities we have—things that are so magical to you—we ghosts and spirits can't do the simple thing that even bacteria and fireflies can do.

DELILAH: Oh. Sad.

(GOPNIK *reads his petition.*)

GOPNIK: "And I demand that you immediately, without any delay, in all possible haste, with the considerable arsenal of laws and powers at your

disposal, I *insist* that you outlaw all communication, communion, congress, consummation, copulation, and/or canoodling between inhabitants of the material world, i.e. the earth, and the spirits and ghosts of other dimensions. Do this for America. Oh, and there's one more thing I insist that you do…"
(He types a few seconds longer, then finishes with:)
—Yours sincerely, Dr Gopnik.
(He hits a key on the typewriter. It goes ding!)

(Fireworks boom in the distance.)

VENEZIO: I think that's why we come back. To gaze at you, the living, with awe. Knowing that you can do, with your amazing and simple bodies, what the angels, with all their terrifying beauty, cannot.

DELILAH: Venezio, I hold on to this belief that I'm crazy and you're a hallucination because if I really believed for a second that you are you, and you're really here with me…well, I wouldn't be able to recover from all that happiness.

VENEZIO: Then think of me any way you want, Delilah—as a ghost, or a memory, or a mirage, or an echo, or an imperfect reflection of a small, imperfect man.

DELILAH: Not so imperfect.

VENEZIO: As long as you let me gaze at you, feel your body heat, and marvel at the endless reproduction of beautiful life in your body, I'll be content.

DELILAH: You are getting me so hot.

(DELILAH and VENEZIO kiss.)

(The sun comes up on a new day.)

(A newspaper flies on stage. GOPNIK catches it and reads.)

GOPNIK: Yes! I love this country!

(GOPNIK runs into the house and startles DELILAH and VENEZIO.)

DELILAH: What are you doing here?

GOPNIK: Sorry but there seems to be a change of plans. *(He reads the newspaper.)* "The unelected junta of the United States of America hereby forbids the presence of the dead within all its fifty-nine states, off-shore colonies, and secret re-education camps, beginning today, and for the rest of all eternity, or until such time as we change our minds yet again."

VENEZIO: What? I'm not allowed to stay...?

GOPNIK: Venezio. My homeboy. Adios.

(Something cool and metaphysical happens...and VENEZIO starts to disappear.)

DELILAH: Venezio...?

VENEZIO: Good-bye again, my Delilah. Remember to live! Remember to love! Remember to be happy! *(He has vanished.)*

(DELILAH pulls the knife from GOPNIK's belt. She cuts her wrist. Great amounts of her blood flow.)

DELILAH: Ha, doctor, ha! I'll soon be joining my man and you can't stop me!

GOPNIK: Oh, and I insisted that they outlaw death again. And the government said yes. You're not going anywhere, *mi amor.*

(DELILAH drops her knife, screams, and passes out.)

(GOPNIK catches DELILAH in his arms.)

(Black out)

END OF ACT THREE

(Intermission)

ACT FOUR

(A few days later)

(GOPNIK's bicycle is parked next to the house. His black doctor bag is on the comfy chair.)

(VENEZIO exists in some colorful distant dimension that makes it impossible for him to communicate with DELILAH or she with him.)

(VENEZIO wears thick dark glasses that make it very hard for him to see DELILAH.)

(DELILAH, dressed as she was in ACT THREE, can't see or hear VENEZIO.)

(DELILAH stands, back against one of the newly-painted walls, facing the audience, somewhat comatose, face blank.)

(DELILAH's wrist is bandaged.)

(GOPNIK enters the stage carrying windows. He puts them on the floor of the house.)

GOPNIK: Windows are on sale at Ikea.

(DELILAH opens her bandages to look at her scars. They seem to fascinate her.)

DELILAH: You almost did it, girl, you almost got there.

(GOPNIK puts the window in various places to see what looks best.)

(VENEZIO strains to see what GOPNIK is doing.)

VENEZIO: What's he *building* in there…?

GOPNIK: Big news! They're opening a farmer's market down the street.

(DELILAH *closes up her bandages.*)

DELILAH: Yeah, almost did it, girl.

(GOPNIK *works through the short, tense silence.*)

GOPNIK: You picked a great location for this house. They say the local schools are the best in the county.

DELILAH: So?

GOPNIK: So—the children! The little Doctor Gopniks and little Delilahs will need good schools!

DELILAH: Hm.

GOPNIK: You'll have to make sure you're telling me when you're ovulating.

DELILAH: What if I don't feel like sharing that particular, intimate piece of information?

GOPNIK: No worries. I wrote a Masters Thesis called "Circadian Rhythms and the Vagina." I'll figure it out eventually.

(DELILAH *is too grossed out to respond.*)

GOPNIK: The re-population of the earth is going well, I hear. There are now Americans in all the countries we invaded, which was all of them. Of course it took a while to remove all the bodies of the people we once called Russians and Thais and Argentines. Lots of pyres and hasty mass graves which we created with our usual Yank efficiency. Did you know that the first structures Columbus built in the New World were gallows? Things haven't really changed all that much, if you think about it.

DELILAH: I don't want to think about it.

GOPNIK: I was thinking that it'd be nice to build an extension to the house, a few more bedrooms for our

young Americans. That's going to mean cutting down
this Tree to make space.

(*The Tree blinks in response.*)

(DELILAH *pauses, and responds as if another knife were
going in her heart…then quickly covers the pain.*)

DELILAH: You can turn it into gallows for all I care,
Doctor Gopnik.

(GOPNIK *stops what he's doing and goes to* DELILAH.)

GOPNIK: My dearest…

DELILAH: I was taking a hot shower this morning. And
I looked at the mirror, all covered in steam. I stared
at it a long time. And I could swear, as the steam
condensed and morphed, that it was forming a face.
Venezio's face. I think he was trying to contact me.

GOPNIK: Have you been taking the meds I've
prescribed?

DELILAH: There was a bird, sitting in our Tree
of Light—the Tree you want so desperately to
assassinate—and the bird made a little song that
sounded like this: *Ven-ETE-zio! Ven-ETE-zio!*

GOPNIK: Those are not messages from the other side…

(GOPNIK *tries to put his arm around* DELILAH.)

(DELILAH *pulls away, looks up at the sky, jumps up and
down, waving her arms in a complicated pattern.*)

DELILAH: I'M RIGHT HERE! HONEY, CAN YOU SEE
ME?! I'M RIGHT DOWN HERE!

VENEZIO: *!Me cago en na'!* What is she doing?
(*He tries to take off his dark glasses but they're stuck to his
head.*)
(*When he touches them, he gets small electric shocks.*)
—Bitch!

DELILAH: You've always been a rebel, don't let this one stupid law keep you from me.

VENEZIO: I CAN'T HEAR YOU! DELILAH! WAVE AT ME IF YOU UNDERSTAND!

(DELILAH *gives up.*)

DELILAH: Buried alive. I am buried alive.

(DELILAH *runs to the radioactive waste. Takes a big gulp of it—nothing happens but pain in her stomach.*)

(GOPNIK *sighs, holds out pills.*)

(DELILAH *takes the pills, sullen, resigned.*)

GOPNIK: Alright, I get it. You still love the guy.

DELILAH: You think I want to keep yearning for him? You think I like feeling like this?

GOPNIK: Grief is like any chemical in the body, Delilah Louise. It needs to take its time to ride through your system and gracefully leave your body.

DELILAH: You only call me Delilah Louise when you're deeply disappointed in me.

VENEZIO: DID YOU HEAR WHAT I SAID??! WAVE YOUR ARMS LIKE THIS!
(*He waves his arms in a complicated pattern.*)

GOPNIK: You're polluted with him. All your blood is saturated with his words and memories. No matter how many times you slash yourself.

DELILAH: I know I'm traumatizing you by acting like this.

GOPNIK: I was trained in blood. That doesn't hurt me. But at night, when I hear you cry. That's what I can't take.

DELILAH: You can hear me from the other room?

GOPNIK: All I want to do is burst in your bedroom and take care of you. To bleed you like an 18th century doctor until all the Venezio inside you is gone.

DELILAH: Why do you stay here then?

GOPNIK: Some day the chemicals of your grief will be replaced by something else. Something I dare not even name. Then you'll realize that the man you should be with is the man who takes care of you.

DELILAH: There's a certain good logic to that.

VENEZIO: I CAN'T HEAR WHAT YOU'RE SAYING BUT REMEMBER THAT IF IT WASN'T FOR HIM I WOULDN'T BE IN THIS LIMBO!

GOPNIK: Then with luck a new chemistry will be written in your cells. And maybe, if I play my cards right, I'll be the one you see in the steam of your mirror.

DELILAH: That's going to take a lot of work on your part. You think I'm worth all that effort?

GOPNIK: I never ask myself that question. Let me look at those wrists.

(GOPNIK *opens his doctor bag and takes out fresh rolls of bandages and gauze. He kisses* DELILAH *scars and re-bandages her wrists.*)

VENEZIO: Oh, what's he doing to her now?

(DELILAH *can't help but look at* GOPNIK *rather tenderly.*)

DELILAH: I just want some peace, you know? A world where death is death again and life is life and the U S government can't change shit on a whim. A world where Americans aren't everywhere, running everything. Where a lover is a lover for life.

GOPNIK: That's a dream world, *mi amor.*

(*Beat*)

DELILAH: Some of that special medicine you gave me last time gave me that dream-world feeling. I closed my eyes and Venezio and I were fencing and playing around like before the world went mad. I would like some more of that medicine, please.

GOPNIK: Delilah, I can't keep pumping you full of drugs.

DELILAH: Please, just a little? I won't tell anyone on you.

GOPNIK: But ethically speaking—

DELILAH: Everything's so much easier when you help me out like that. Everything's so sweet. Come on, be a mensch.

(GOPNIK *hesitates.*)

GOPNIK: Will you promise this will be the last time?

DELILAH: Oh, I promise, sir.

GOPNIK: You're a pretty good liar, you know that?

DELILAH: You know you can't say no to me, so don't even pretend you can.

(*Knowing this is true,* GOPNIK *opens his doctor bag and takes out a syringe.*)

DELILAH: I love you for doing this, you know.

GOPNIK: I wish you loved me for better reasons than this.

(GOPNIK *examines* DELILAH's *arm for a vein, finds one, and gives her an injection.*)

(DELILAH *gasps, soft and low.*)

(*In a few seconds, the drug kicks in and a serene look comes over* DELILAH's *face.*)

(GOPNIK *gets closer to her, puts his arm around her.*)

DELILAH: Don't think this is going to get you laid, dear doctor.

(GOPNIK *pulls away.*)

GOPNIK: I wouldn't presume.

DELILAH: Come here, you oafish man!

(DELILAH *puts her arms around* GOPNIK *and holds him.*)

VENEZIO: Are they making out?

DELILAH: Hm, this is much nicer, isn't it?

GOPNIK: Are you feeling better?

DELILAH: If I can't kill myself anymore, I suppose this weird deadening cloud in my brain is the next best thing.

VENEZIO: This is a fiasco. If I could just get back to her. Take off these damn dark glasses!
(*He struggles with the glasses again but they don't come off.*)
(*More electric shocks—stronger.*)
—Bitch, bitch!

DELILAH: I don't feel any regrets right now. I don't miss Venezio, or care about finishing the house, or saving the Tree or stress that they're going to change their stupid laws again and make my life hell.

(GOPNIK *holds* DELILAH *tighter.*)

VENEZIO: That's it! This is intolerable!
(*He struggles to leave his dimension and come closer to the house.*)

DELILAH: Connecting to him…what was I doing? Connecting to some childhood dream? A first crush? A first kiss under a magic Tree in the spring? A first realization that maybe, on this long journey in this wicked world, you don't have to walk alone? There's a partner, a shadow, a guide who takes the trip with you and keeps the sun from shining too hot and pulls out the weeds in your path? What was all that but the naive yearning and illusion of youth? Who needs that crapola?

(VENEZIO *stops, suddenly very afraid.*)

VENEZIO: What am I doing? I can't break the law!

DELILAH: He never wanted me. I pushed marriage on him. I sent out the pink invitations and dragged him into an adulthood he wasn't ready for.

GOPNIK: Shhhhhhhhhhh.

VENEZIO: The laws of heaven and earth are horrible. The punishments, they say, are dreadful. Everyone obeys, no matter what.
(*He cowers like a beaten dog.*)

DELILAH: It used to get me so mad. Now? I don't really feel it any more...

GOPNIK: I guess that's good.

DELILAH: I feel milky and soft and vague and free. And it's all because of the little magic medicines in the little magic bag of little magic Doctor Gopnik. Can I have another? Please?

GOPNIK: But you just said—

DELILAH: Please? Please?

GOPNIK: But I don't think that's such a good...

(DELILAH *goes to the cowering* VENEZIO *and looks at him.*)

DELILAH: Sometimes I think I see him. Somewhere in a dimly-lit dimension where they warehouse the dead, all in their rags, smelling like rot, begging the universe for some spare change and bread. Please, I don't think I want to have this vision any more.

GOPNIK: As a man of Hippocrates and Aristotle, I hesitate...

DELILAH: Just one more. To dull the visions. Make the smell of death go away. To make me softer and lighter. I think maybe one more little shot will make it quite possible for a sad medicine man we both know to get laid tonight.

GOPNIK: Oh, well.

(GOPNIK *gives* DELILAH *another injection. It immediately clouds her senses and personality.*)

DELILAH: Aaaaaahhhhhhhhh...that's a really good shot ...

(*Night falls with a heavy audible thud.*)

(*The moon looks like a disfigured green, dripping smudge in the sky, almost unrecognizable as the moon.*)

(DELILAH *stands, looks around at the unfinished house.*)

DELILAH: This house was supposed to be my salvation. I planned it out so perfectly. Ha! Our silly plans!
(*Beat*)
Bedroom?

GOPNIK: That way.

DELILAH: You have the eyes of a dying puppy dog. Eyes that ask for love and pity.

GOPNIK: I have the Mediterranean in me.

DELILAH: Which one will you get tonight from me, old friend—love or pity?

GOPNIK: I don't have enough pride to choose between them.

DELILAH: Yes, dear, you'll take whatever you can get from me tonight.

(DELILAH *takes* GOPNIK's *hand.*)

(VENEZIO *groans.*)

GOPNIK & VENEZIO: Delilah.

(DELILAH *starts to pull* GOPNIK *to the upstage bedroom.*)

(GOPNIK *unexpectedly resists and pulls away.*)

(DELILAH *looks at* GOPNIK *and laughs.*)

DELILAH: Outbreak of scruples, doctor?

GOPNIK: I don't want to love you all full of drugs like this. You're not you this way. It feels false and stolen and forced—

DELILAH: It's *sex*, Gopnik. *Sex.*

GOPNIK: Yeah good point.

(DELILAH *laughs and pulls* GOPNIK *to the bedroom entrance.*)

DELILAH: I think I need a full-body examination. *Full*, doctor, without the gloves.

(GOPNIK *looks at* DELILAH *knowing it's impossible for him to resist her.*)

GOPNIK: You make me grateful I studied medicine and learned its ineffable mysteries.

(DELILAH *and* GOPNIK *disappear in the off-stage bedroom.*)

(*Blinded by the dark glasses, afraid to touch them,* VENEZIO *stumbles around his dimension.*)

VENEZIO: These are the facts, Delilah. You blow my mind. No one can touch you for loveliness and melancholy. My nerves sizzle when you come. You write new definitions for goodness. I was afraid of the love-struggle. Until I realized I love the struggle and I hate the struggle and I love the struggle. I was afraid to be captured but I didn't understand what a tender owner you'd be. How well you'd take care of your wayward, lost, and distracted lover.

(*As* VENEZIO *stumbles and falls on his face, the sun comes up on the next day.*)

(DELILAH, *still in black, enters from the off-stage bedroom. Though the drugs have worn off and she's more her old self, she looks like she's had a rough night.*)

DELILAH: This can't be happening to me…

(VENEZIO *gets to his feet. His hands out like a blind man, he stumbles across the stage.*)

VENEZIO: Delilah? Delilah?

(VENEZIO *leaves the stage.*)

(DELILAH *goes to the Tree of Light and talks to it.*)

DELILAH: You're the only one of your kind, you know that, Tree? Planted in an old playground where little wars were fought, little truces signed, little love affairs flared like small diamonds. I thought it would be the perfect place for a Tree. Then a house. Then a life.

(*The Tree blinks in response.*)

(DELILAH *tries to keep focused, strong.*)

DELILAH: Things got a little out of hand last night. I was empty like a porcelain cup and Doctor Gopnik came into the room and filled me up. Oh—there's no way to describe the awful dreams created by the collision of your drugs and your fears.
(*Beat, as she looks at the Tree in sad silence.*)
He says he's the master of the house now because last night he took possession of me and whatever he says is the law and that this will be your last day with me because he's going to chop you down after breakfast and send you to be turned into toilet paper and napkins.

(GOPNIK, *wearing a guayabera, comes out of the bedroom with an axe. Something very fundamental has changed in him since sleeping with* DELILAH.)

GOPNIK: Where's my breakfast?

DELILAH: In a minute, dear.

GOPNIK: I'll need some fuel for the execution and wanton destruction of this perfectly harmless and amazingly beautiful living thing.

DELILAH: You've changed a lot since we slept together.

GOPNIK: What do you expect? You made me wait too long. I felt like I finally climbed Mount Everest and the thing about climbing Mount Everest is after you've climbed Mount Everest you kinda hate Mount Everest.

DELILAH: Funny, I'd think after climbing Mount Everest you'd kind of *respect* Mount Everest.

GOPNIK: It's got to be easier tonight, you hear me?

DELILAH: I'll do my best, sir.

GOPNIK: Maybe a little more enthusiasm would help.

DELILAH: I was drugged out of my mind last night.

GOPNIK: Is that your excuse?

DELILAH: It's the only excuse I have for letting you sleep with me in the first place.

GOPNIK: Hey, I let *you* sleep with *me* because you were a goddamn basket-case, got it?

DELILAH: Yes, of course, I don't know why I'm remembering everything all wrong, sir. I just have to ask you something, though ...

(DELILAH *goes to* GOPNIK *and takes his hand.*)

GOPNIK: Hand-holding is a prelude to manipulation.

DELILAH: I just wonder, Doctor Gopnik, why can't you be *nice* Doctor Gopnik like you used to be?

GOPNIK: I *hate* that old Doctor Gopnik. Whining and begging just so you'd pay attention to him. Reminding him that he's never going to measure up to Venezio.

DELILAH: I guess I was very mean to you.

GOPNIK: It embarrasses me to even think about it.
That's why there are new rules around here, a change
of attitude. And I think to reinforce my point, I'm
going to make you chop down the Tree and get rid of it
yourself.

(GOPNIK *hands* DELILAH *the axe.*)

DELILAH: Me?
(*She takes the axe and looks at the gorgeous Tree.*)
(*A long moment of paralysis*)
(*She puts the axe down and tries not to cry.*)
I want the drugs again, Doctor Gopnik. I want them
right now and I want them extra-strength. No, actually,
I want *death*, I want *out of here*, I want to find my
Venezio in that other place. But I can't have that, can
I? So fill me up, Doctor Gopnik, with those chemical
shock-troops in your black bag. If you ever hope to
touch me again, you'll fry my goddamn mind to a
cinder, you understand me? Because you will never
love me or have me or own me or know me *any other
way.*

(GOPNIK *turns away from* DELILAH *and tries not to cry.*)

(*But* GOPNIK *can't stop himself. He cries like a lost boy.*)

GOPNIK: I know that I won't!

(DELILAH, *amazed, goes to* GOPNIK.)

DELILAH: I know it was you who got the laws changed
that sent Venezio's ghost away.

GOPNIK: I was stupid. That's the problem with the
over-educated. We're so goddamn stupid!

DELILAH: I know you did it for your own uncanny
reasons.

GOPNIK: I'm sorry about this morning—acting so
macho. I'm just not used to all this testosterone
running through me. Last night was a huge shock to

my system, you know. It was, well, really nice, Delilah. The happiest night of my life, in fact, the culmination of a dream, even though you were completely drugged up and I did feel vaguely like I was taking advantage of you.

DELILAH: I won't tell anyone. Under one condition. *(She goes to* GOPNIK's *bag and takes out a syringe.)* Go now and search your endless knowledge of pharmaceutical voodoo and concoct for me the strongest, most potent, brain-killing, motherfucker of a drug you can. I want to go *under*, Doctor Gopnik—*all the way under*, and I don't want to come back. Ever. I don't want to see or hear or feel another moment of this life again. I want my memories burned off like an old tattoo, my identity nullified like a bad marriage, and my personality canceled like a sitcom. After you put me down…whatever you do to my limp, comatose body of a sexual nature—whatever you want to stick into whatever hole—well, I don't really give a shit.

*(*DELILAH *gives* GOPNIK *the syringe.)*

*(*GOPNIK *looks at* DELILAH *a long moment.)*

GOPNIK: That's a living death.

DELILAH: Nothing else will make me happy.

(There's a silent beat as GOPNIK *makes his decision.)*

GOPNIK: Okay. Wait for me in the bedroom.

DELILAH: You're really going to help me out?

GOPNIK: I'll be in there in ten minutes.

DELILAH: You're my savior.

*(*DELILAH *throws her arms around* GOPNIK *and kisses him.)*

*(*DELILAH *exits into the bedroom.)*

(Alone, GOPNIK takes a deep breath. He tosses the syringe away and goes over to the magic typewriter. It glows brightly.)

(GOPNIK starts a letter.)

GOPNIK: "Dear Assholes in the Gov-ern-ment…"
(He types fast: he's on fire, tears streaming down his face.)

(Black out)

END OF ACT FOUR

ACT FIVE

(We're in an alternate dimension.)

(The Tree sparkles with colored lights.)

(The sky, the clouds, the ground, everything is colorful.)

(The moon is round, healthy, and turquoise.)

(The sound of hummingbirds.)

(The typewriter, toxic waste barrels and other industrial debris are gone.)

(DELILAH enters.)

(DELILAH's clothes are crazy colors. She wears big, thick dark glasses that make it hard for her to see. She walks around, irresistibly drawn to the Tree of Light.)

(DELILAH tries hard to see the lights on the Tree. She reaches out, takes one of the lights from the Tree, and eats it.)

DELILAH: Yum! Venezio wasn't kidding! You can taste the light!

(She pulls at the glasses but can't take them off.)

(Gets an electric shock)

—Bitch!

(Thunder and lightning are accompanied by violins)

(Soft wind blows. DELILAH opens her mouth. She can taste the wind.)

DELILAH: Oh my God, non-fat vanilla wind with a hint of cloves...*yum!*

(She wanders around the stage, adjusting to the light and gravity of this new dimension.)

But which way is the world? I need to see what's going on with Doctor Gopnik. He did me such a favor. He got the law changed for me. He got the government to bring back death. I need to thank him for that.

(Beat, realizes)

Oh, yeah. That's illegal. Shit!

(She stops. An amazing sensation seizes her.)

Whoa! I know what the sky is thinking! I can read its amazing thoughts!

(She looks up at the sky.)

Hey, sky! Do you know where I can find my Venezio? He was my one true love on earth. Bout yea big, nice eyes, way too cute for his own good. There were miscommunications. We used the same language, but we were using alternative definitions to the words we spoke. It's a male/female thing down on earth. You'd think, after millions of years of evolution, we would have worked it out by now, but that's the way it goes. There's great progress in all fields of human endeavor except in the fields of love. Looks like we're still stuck in some reptile age of the heart.

(A lyre improvises an ancient melody.)

*(*DELILAH *smiles—sees the music dancing in front of her. She dances with it.)*

DELILAH: But! Now that I'm away from the place governed by day and night and gravity and sunlight and cause and effect, I think there may be hope for us. Out here, in this awesome new dimension where all the senses get tangled up to make new rules…I think there's hope for Delilah and Venezio and our reptile hearts.

(Wind, laughter, whale music, the sound of an ice cream truck.)

(The Tree's lights spell the word "Love" in bright pulsing colors.)

(Day and night co-exist.)

DELILAH: But! What if there are as many places to be dead as there are people who die? And we're each exiled to our own lonely heaven and I'm in, like, Dimension 803.6 and he's in, like, Dimension 47-X and the space between us is light years across, and full of inhospitable thieves and ruffians? What if he's married to someone else—some real skank bimbo ho', that's just his type too—or he's too old to remember me or he hates my guts for sleeping with Doctor Gopnik—*even though I was totally drugged the whole time and don't remember a single moment of it*—or he just doesn't care and he's over me? Is that what's going to happen to me? Can I have a little guidance here? Can I have a sign?

(The lights on the Tree change and spell the word "Yes.")

(Doesn't matter since DELILAH can't see it.)

(There's the sound of people making love.)

(DELILAH listens, turned on and annoyed.)

DELILAH: Stop! Too many memories in that sound! I remember it in too many of my limbs and blood vessels.

(The sound of love making abruptly stops.)

DELILAH: I gotta find my boy. I'm going to be here an eternity. Plenty of time. Venezio? Venezio, baby? Are you there?
(She stumbles across the stage and exits.)

(The word "Yes" on the Tree of Light disappears.)

(VENEZIO enters, wearing dark glasses.)

VENEZIO: I don't know what's going on. Every time I look down on our house, Delilah, I don't see you.

I'm afraid something terrible's happened. Have you moved? Are you sick? Have you found someone else, fallen in love and gotten married? I thought I saw Doctor Gopnik in front of our Tree, rolling around on the ground, crying, and pulling his hair out. I hope the old boy's okay. He's so strange.

(A polar bear growls, falcons screech, sound of flames.)

VENEZIO: I'm just going to have to pretend that you're here with me and we can talk to each other and I can tell you about my day and you can tell me what intellectual conquest you've made and what new room you've built in our house and how Buster and Jennifer are progressing through all their awesome stages of life. You can describe the moon to me and tell me how safe I am in this home we've made on the frontier between war and peace, creation and destruction. You always seemed to yearn for the end of the world. We found the end of the world in our house, my dear, just exactly as you wanted.

(He stumbles across the stage, going stage L.)

(The Tree of Light spells out the word "Wait.")

(VENEZIO sniffs the air.)

VENEZIO: Crazy. I think I can smell Delilah's thoughts. Damn she was smart! But that can't be possible…

(He is about to leave the stage.)

(The word "Wait" on the Tree flashes: "Wait Wait Wait Wait.")

(VENEZIO leaves the stage.)

(The Tree of Light spells out the words "Oh, Jesus.")

(DELILAH enters. She walks in backwards, comes to the center of the stage.)

(VENEZIO enters, also walking backwards to the center of the stage.)

(Neither DELILAH *nor* VENEZIO *has any awareness that the other is on stage.)*

(The Tree of Light returns to normal, just waiting, hoping.)

*(*DELILAH *and* VENEZIO *each come to center stage, backs to each other.)*

DELILAH: The after-life is exhausting! So much space to cover and all of it is round and fat like the number seven!

(She lies down on stage to sleep.)

VENEZIO: Funny...on my tongue is a rather ironic tone of voice.

DELILAH: Funny...dancing on my fingertips: a rather literal tone of voice.

VENEZIO: Spicy!

DELILAH: Velvety!

VENEZIO: Must be my imagination.

DELILAH: No, I'm dreaming again.

*(*VENEZIO *stands, starts to walk away, stumbles over* DELILAH *and falls on his face.)*

(Startled, DELILAH *sits up.)*

*(*DELILAH *and* VENEZIO *are face to face—but they can't see each other through the dark glasses.)*

(Wind, coyotes, and babies howl.)

VENEZIO: Shit! Sorry, sorry!

DELILAH: Why don't you watch where you're going, buster?

VENEZIO: Hey, I said I was sorry!

DELILAH: I'm trying to sleep here—

VENEZIO: Well maybe you shouldn't be sleeping where other people are walking.

DELILAH: Why isn't there a gendarme with a nightstick around when you need one?

VENEZIO: Look, I'll get out of your way, you don't have to worry about that, I don't need this crap, you know, rude, crazy nut-job.

DELILAH: Who are you calling a rude, crazy nut-job? If I had a fencing foil I would teach you a lesson!

VENEZIO: Yeah? Well, maybe you should check your map 'cause I think you took a wrong turn on your way to hell!

(DELILAH *and* VENEZIO *both stand, face each other, ready for a fight, even though they can't see.*)

(DELILAH *and* VENEZIO *shadow box—really meaning to hit each other, but missing wildly…until they slowly subside.*)

DELILAH: I don't know who you are, but I'm getting a minor volcanic eruption in all my lymph nodes and in the back of my knees because of you!

VENEZIO: And I'm being blasted with mosaics and sensational whirligigs in the weird folds under my tongue and elbows, because of you, no doubt!

(*Motionless,* DELILAH *and* VENEZIO *face each other, a little overwhelmed by the feelings they're getting.*)

DELILAH: The tips of my hair are picking up buzzing electrical signals from you in strange parabolas.

VENEZIO: The water in my eyes is now orange-flavored and I think some cowboy ballad is playing in my spine.

DELILAH: Why are you doing this to me, stranger? Why are you puzzling my body memories and flooding my mouth with triangles and mint chocolate?

VENEZIO: I could ask you the same thing! When I first got here, it took me a long time to get used to the crazy way your senses get re-arranged. But this is something totally new…

DELILAH: Tell me about it! I don't think I'm used to it yet. But it's really—well, except for the disturbing smells in my inner-ear, because of *you* no doubt—I don't really hate it...

VENEZIO: Yeah...I'm even liking the vertigo in my lungs: caused, no doubt, by you.

DELILAH: Yeah, well, that's life. Or death. Or whatever this condition is—if "is" is the word that adequately describes this moment and the situation we're in, whatever that is—if "is" is the word that applies to the situation we're in, let alone the condition which gave rise to the situation in the first place, whatever that is—or was—or, oh God, I am exhausting myself.

(Beat)

VENEZIO: So. Did you just get here? Are you new?

DELILAH: Fresh off the boat—or the spaceship—or the giant green sea turtle—or whatever it was ...

VENEZIO: How did you...?

DELILAH: Official cause of death: a broken heart.

VENEZIO: Me too. Wow. God, you. You, uh...seem so damn...your polka-dotted voice...and the purple swirl around your breathing...

DELILAH: Weird, you're making me hear this navy-blue melody in my medulla oblongata.

VENEZIO: Without seeing you, I can tell—despite your short temper and tendency to see all of existence as an over-analyzed *lucha libre*—that you're, well, not a bad person at all.

DELILAH: It's probably some clever sensory manipulation on your part. But I get a good vibe in my pituitary gland and along my pancreas about you too, as well as deep in my...

(The feeling she is getting from him intensifies.)

...oh, my! Oh, *well!*

(Then VENEZIO *gets it.)*

VENEZIO: What? Are you feeling what I'm—? *Ay!*

DELILAH: I seem to be getting very good intelligence that you are inventive and playful in the bedroom department.

VENEZIO: I can't believe you're saying that! I'm getting the same hit on you.

*(*DELILAH *and* VENEZIO *both stand there, highly turned on, a little embarrassed, but giggling.)*

DELILAH: Maybe that's what makes this Heaven. Every person you meet, even if you've never met them before...you understand their goodness in the deepest possible way.

VENEZIO: Right, you know their sorrows, their needs and every secret thing that makes them unique...

DELILAH: No judgements, just a pure drinking in of all the ways another person is beautiful.

VENEZIO: That would be paradise.

*(*DELILAH *smiles at this thought.)*

DELILAH: I've only known one other person on earth who's ever given me this feeling.

VENEZIO: I used to be flooded every day with the excess joy of her heart. But the trouble was...I never knew how to hold it all in my hands...

DELILAH: And when you finally figured it out, it was too late.

VENEZIO: How do you know?

DELILAH: I have that same story, in reverse, with a pain-in-the-ass boy with mambos and Mozart coming out of his eyes.

VENEZIO: God, what I wouldn't give for a chance to tell her, really *tell* her...

DELILAH: God, there are so many things I would have liked to hear my boy say to me. Before the twilight came and it was too late.

VENEZIO: I sense that in my feet.

(Short silence)

DELILAH: Well. It's been nice meeting you. This dimension is strangely under-populated.

VENEZIO: I think most people are at the Party Dimension. I hear it's loud there.

DELILAH: Parties are not for me.

VENEZIO: Me neither. I think I'd rather just sit in a big comfy chair and have quiet conversations about nothing and everything—then have hot sex.

DELILAH: Yes...yes...hm...

(Beat)

Well, my friend, I'm on a quest. I'm looking for that pain-in-the-ass boy. I'm determined to visit every dimension in the universe until I find him, even if I have to slay Orcs and Morlocks to do it.

VENEZIO: Then I won't keep you.

DELILAH: This has been a very sweet conversation. I mean that literally. Your words are raspberries and cumin.

VENEZIO: Yours are fuchsia and with a hint of excess cherry lollipops.

(DELILAH starts to leave, then hesitates.)

DELILAH: I have to tell you that I sense...God, it's just you've got so much sadness in you. Layers of regret. They go so far down. I don't know how you can even talk.

VENEZIO: I know. I hold on to stuff. It's been a problem for me. And you. There's so much guilt in there...

DELILAH: Yes, I hurt someone. An old friend. He was a dear, kind, over-educated medicine man with twinkly little eyeballs, and too much Aristotle, who loved me so fiercely and taught me so much. And I killed his heart.

VENEZIO: I get the feeling he never stopped loving you. I mean, how could anyone?

(DELILAH *and* VENEZIO *hold out their hands. In their blindness, it takes them a moment to find each other's hands. When they do, they shake hands.*)

(DELILAH *and* VENEZIO *turn around to face opposite directions, ready to leave.*)

(*The Tree of Light spells words in rapid succession: "I'm." "Going." "To." "Kill." "You." "Both."*)

(DELILAH *and* VENEZIO *walk to opposite ends of the stage.*)

(*Right before exiting,* DELILAH *and* VENEZIO *stop.*)

DELILAH: I know what you taste, smell, sound, and feel like. I would love to know what you look like.

VENEZIO: I'd love that too.

(*Suddenly* DELILAH *and* VENEZIO *run to center stage from opposite sides and almost knock each other down when they collide.*)

DELILAH: So, tell me, what's up with these stupid glasses?

VENEZIO: So that we don't see the living.

DELILAH: But we're not the living, we're the other guys, the dearly departed.

VENEZIO: Look, the people who make the laws are idiots, period. Even out here.

(*The sound of Pink Floyd-ish maniacal laughter*)

DELILAH: So if we want to see each other, we're going to have to take them off.

VENEZIO: I've been trying to get mine off since I got here, but the shocks are killing me.

DELILAH: It's a conundrum.

VENEZIO: Unsolvable! We're doomed!

DELILAH: ...no, wait, okay...just a thought, okay? ...But what if...you can't take off your own glasses, right? ... Because of some obscure, stupid rule...but you *can* take off the glasses that *other people* are wearing!

VENEZIO: That makes no sense. Why would that work?

DELILAH: Don't you even want to try?

VENEZIO: Seems like a waste of time and effort to me. Just ridiculous.

DELILAH: I sense you're the kind of person who pretends to be a rebel but really plays it safe.

VENEZIO: I sense you're the kind of person who tells people the truth when they really don't want to hear it.

DELILAH: Hey, let's just try this, okay? You reach out to take off my glasses and I'll reach out to take yours.

VENEZIO: Okay. But it's never going to work. It's just going to lead to raised expectations followed by the train crash of dashed hope.

DELILAH: COME ON, JUST DO IT!

VENEZIO: On three.

DELILAH: One, two...

(DELILAH *and* VENEZIO *tentatively reach out for each other...*)

(*...The sound of tornadoes, landslides, galaxies crashing... growing, growing...*)

VENEZIO: *Oh shit...!*

DELILAH: *I don't like the sound of that…!*

VENEZIO: *Are you sure you want to keep going?*

DELILAH: *YES! I do!!*

VENEZIO: *OKAY!! Me too!!*

(*…Hands trembling,* DELILAH *and* VENEZIO *touch each other's dark glasses…*)

(*…The noise hits a terrifying peak…*)

(*…*DELILAH *and* VENEZIO *scream!*)

DELILAH & VENEZIO: *HOLY SHIIIIIIIIIIIIIIIIIIIIIIIIIITT!!*

(*Their dark glasses come off…easily.*)

(*Silence*)

(*Now that they can see,* DELILAH *and* VENEZIO *quickly look around at the colorful space surrounding them.*)

DELILAH: Wow, it's wild and pretty up here.

VENEZIO: We get the craziest weather. It snows mathematical equations, square roots, and cannolis.

(DELILAH *and* VENEZIO *look at each other a long moment.*)

(DELILAH *and* VENEZIO *are surprised but not surprised to see each other.*)

DELILAH: Oh my God, there are bells in your heart and they feel like gold.

VENEZIO: Down in my stomach, I think I can hear the amber in your eyes.

(*Without a word,* DELILAH *and* VENEZIO *throw themselves on each other and hug and kiss and jump up and down like happy, amazed children, screaming and laughing.*)

DELILAH: I found you! I can't believe I found you! Oh, Venezio, my Venezio…oh, I missed you so much!

VENEZIO: Don't say that or my hair will collapse and I won't be able to breathe.

DELILAH: I would rather hold you than breathe!

(They hold each other.)

VENEZIO: God, it's you. It's my Delilah. So how've you been?

DELILAH: Dead. I've been dead.

VENEZIO: Yeah, me too. But I feel good, don't you?

DELILAH: Yeah, I feel great now. And I guess the big question is—are we going to live together out here? I see a house, just like our old house. Except someone actually finished this one. Is that house for us?

VENEZIO: If we want it, I guess.

DELILAH: Do you want it? Will you yearn for something else when you're with me—stuck with obsessive-compulsive, head-strong, anal-compulsive, compulsively anal, stubbornly obsessive, over-analytical me for an eternity?

VENEZIO: Wow, fuck.

DELILAH: Hey!

(VENEZIO laughs.)

VENEZIO: But I think that being with each other doesn't mean the end of yearning. We can be with each other and still yearn and grieve for the things that hurt and separate us. Still miss each other when we're only a moment away.

(DELILAH and VENEZIO take each other's hands. Then they hold each other.)

(Comets, supernovas, spinning rings of Saturn cruise the sky.)

(It snows mathematical formulas and sonnets.)

DELILAH: Well. This is our existence now. In a multicolored dimension with some real crazy-ass weather. But does that mean we're really supposed to be happy now? Without conflict, can we really feel joyful? Don't we need its opposite to appreciate the thing we have? Doesn't every action have to have an equal and opposite reaction?

VENEZIO: Delilah, man—you are such a drag sometimes!

DELILAH: And you're still a pain-in-the-ass boy!

(DELILAH *and* VENEZIO *run off in opposite directions.*)

(DELILAH *and* VENEZIO *come back, holding fencing foils.*)

(DELILAH *and* VENEZIO *face off, salute each other, and begin to fence.*)

(VENEZIO *gets the first hit.*)

VENEZIO: I got you!

DELILAH: No you didn't! You'll never get me! Not in all the eternities in all the worlds to come!

(DELILAH *and* VENEZIO *fence.*)

(DELILAH *gets* VENEZIO *in the heart.*)

VENEZIO: Ayyy! Yeah! That's a really good shot!

DELILAH: Does it hurt? Are you in terrible pain?

VENEZIO: Yes I am. I'm in terrible pain.

(DELILAH *smiles, full of love.*)

DELILAH: The worst pain there is.

(DELILAH *and* VENEZIO *continue to fence.*)

(GOPNIK *enters in colorful clothes and rides his multi-colored bicycle in circles around them—and spicy constellations spin from his wheels.*)

(*Blackout*)

END OF PLAY

www.ingramcontent.com/pod-product-compliance
Lightning Source LLC
Chambersburg PA
CBHW070024110426
42741CB00034B/2528